CW00497836

Living in the Moment

**The Sayings & Wisdom of
Epiah Khan.**

**Introduced
by
Chris Parker**

Chiselbury

Published by Chiselbury Publishing, a division of Woodstock Leasor Limited
14 Devonia Road, London N1 8JH

www.chiselbury.com

ISBN: 978-1-916556-00-3

'It starts before it starts.
It ends after it ends.'

Epiah Khan

A brief introduction to Epiah Khan

His life

Epiah Khan is an apocryphal Middle Eastern mystic and martial artist who lived in London from 1907 to 1913. Much of his life before this time is shrouded in mystery. However, it is likely that Epiah was born in Baghdad in or around 1860.

Founded in AD 762 by the Abbasid caliph al-Mansur, Baghdad benefitted significantly from its trade-friendly position on the river Tigris close to the Euphrates. Within two hundred years it had become a centre for science, the arts, philosophy and religion, and was regarded by the ninth century historian Yaqubi as the potential 'crossroads of the Universe.'[1]

Epiah was drawn to spiritual study from an early age and would undoubtedly have been influenced by the great teachers living in the city. From the few insights available to us we can glean that, as the years passed, Epiah spent increasing amounts of time alone, meditating and praying in the nearby countryside. Eventually he was drawn to assume the role of the travelling teacher.

Thus, we can see him following in the tradition of many of the world's great mystics, making the transition from formal study under the guidance of an established Guru to a period of self-imposed isolation, learning alone in nature, before

---

[1] Kitab al-Buldan by Yaqubi, Ahmad ibn Abi Yaqub, d. 897?; Juynboll, Abrahamus Wilhelmus Theodorus, 1833-1887

returning to share his wisdom with others.

During his six years in London, Epiah attracted a handful of disciples keen to study his mix of holistic martial arts and intense mystical practice. He also attracted the attention of Katherine Mansfield. She was a poet and writer who served as Assistant Editor of Rhythm, a literary, arts and critical review magazine. Katherine interviewed Epiah, presumably with the intention of writing an essay about him. Sadly, it was never published as the magazine went out of print in 1913. An extract from the original interview is included in this introduction.

It is within the interview that Epiah refers to his home as a *round city* and makes reference to the fact that the city walls were destroyed. These comments imply that the city in question was Baghdad, as al-Mansur's design was circular, and the city's walls were brought down in 1870. However, Epiah favoured the use of metaphor in both his writing and speech, so his references to *the circle* and the *destruction of the walls* need not be taken literally.

Although seemingly settled in London, Epiah moved abruptly and without warning to Paris in the Spring of 1913. From there he travelled to Verdun just before the start of the First World War. His last writings were dated April 16th 1916, less than seven weeks after the start of the battle intended to 'bleed France white'.[2] It is presumed that he died

---

[2] The quote is attributed to Erich von Falkenhayn, the German Chief of Staff. The siege of Verdun was the longest battle of the First World War. More than 250,000 people died and over 500,000 were wounded. The French won. Falkenhayn was removed as Chief of Staff. Epiah Khan disappeared.

during the fighting and that his body was never identified.

His writing

Epiah Khan's sayings and poetry reflect both the insights and wisdom achieved through a lifetime of contemplative study, and an acute awareness of the limitation of words in sharing the deepest realities of human experience. Hence his extensive use of metaphor, challenging the reader to dwell *in the space around the words* with the aim of uncovering ever-deeper layers of meaning. In this way, he reminds us that the greatest truths can only be shared through either myth or metaphor.

I became aware of, and responsible for, the entire collection of Epiah's writing over twenty-five years ago. In that time his influence has reached out into all aspects of my life and work.

The sayings that follow are just a sample of the many he left behind and are presented in the order in which they appear in his original manuscripts. I have resisted the temptation to group them in ways that highlight the recurring themes and progressive insights he offers.

As Epiah makes clear in his interview with Katherine Mansfield, individual sayings should not be considered in isolation; however, the sequencing of his work allows us to make this mistake. By deliberately disguising this essential connectivity, Epiah develops his challenge to the reader. His underlying message is that everything is relational, even though this is not immediately obvious. Our task – in life as in reading his work - is to recognise these relationships and our role within them. The question is, 'Do we have the desire – the motivation – to connect the dots?'

And Epiah seems comfortable and accepting of the fact that for many of us the answer is, 'No, I'm too busy getting through today to have time for such thoughtful – or, perhaps, even, thoughtless – reflection. Today, the best I can do is accept what he is saying on the level that is most obvious to me. Maybe there will be a time, another day, another stage in my life, when I can explore the space around the words more deeply.'

Epiah Khan offers the assurance that there will be. His words are a gift. They are ours to do with as we please, as and when we can. They are waiting for us to revisit them whenever it feels right to do so. They offer themselves as a constant, never-ending well; a well we can dip into according to the changes and learning we experience as we move through our own precious lifecycle.

Not surprisingly, given the time Epiah spent alone outside the city, the role of nature as a teacher is a central theme. He uses it to tease us into accepting the fact that we are as much a part of nature as the river, or the flower, or the night sky. We are, therefore, our own natural teachers. We can learn from the brilliantly complex relationship between our brain, mind, and body, at least as much as we can from all other parts of the interconnected natural world.

Other themes Epiah gives equal prominence to include: the Circular nature of existence; Space and Silence and their relationship with Looking and Listening; the negative influences of the Ego (he refers to it as *the Second Self*); the mystery of Love and the absolute importance of Breath.

In our modern world, with fingertip access to all human learning, it is seductively easy to compare the writing of Epiah Khan to those of other well-known mystics. Whilst his warning about the danger of comparison might help us resist the temptation, I find it easy to imagine him smiling as we struggle with that and the many other distractions that come between us and living in the moment.

Meeting with a mystic

The following is an extract of an interview transcript dated January 1913. The interviewer is Katherine Mansfield. The subject is Epiah Khan.

KM: Thank you for agreeing to talk to me today. At Rhythm magazine we believe that freedom, reality, and individuality are three names for the ultimate essence of life. They are the three qualities of the artist. Do you agree?

EK: Freedom is certainly the first of all prisons. (Smiles.) By which I mean we have more space in which to grow than we can possibly imagine. The challenge that presents is two-fold. Firstly, we have to acknowledge this and behave accordingly. Secondly, we have to avoid filling that space with those things that are purely man-made. If we fail to do either of these, we draw our prison walls ever closer around us. Thus, it becomes reasonable to ask those who cry out for freedom, or argue loudly about its value, 'From whom, or what, do you seek to be free?' If it is only from the influence and authority of others, the answer is simple: turn your attention away from them and into the space that is your birth right.
As for reality and individuality, we must also be rigorous in our response. What reality are we referring to? Is it the reality of our own creation, or that which precedes and surrounds us and asks nothing more than we learn how to look and listen? Is it the reality of the city or the reality of the desert? Is it the reality of our first breath or our last? I would suggest that once we have experienced the original nature of reality, we inevitably release our grip on the need for comparison. At that point the concept of individuality dissolves into the wind as we begin to recognise the relationships that connect all

aspects of Life. Nothing exists in isolation - no living being, no movement or thought, no verse of poetry or saying, no community or country. Ultimately, we are as one.

KM: We also believe that the artist is intimate and at one with all he meets. He is in love with life. He has all the careless self-surrender of the lover. As a mystic and a martial artist, do you recognise that as a description of yourself?

EK: There is nothing careless about the practice of either contemplation or martial arts. However, both can be all consuming, just as the lover is consumed by their desire and longing. The difference, though, between the love of the mystic and that of the physical lover is a profound one. Whilst both seek union, mystics seek to lose themself completely in the Other. They require neither gratification nor reward. Their love comes from a source the conscious mind cannot fathom. It is a love that is present in everyone and yet is often covered by the debris of our social structures and symbols. It is a love that can only be revealed when the person is truly present.

KM: How is this achieved?

EK: Through surrender and weakness. The oneness you referred to in your previous question cannot be known whilst the 'I' of isolation dominates our thoughts. This 'I' is the Second Self. It is the 'I' of our own creation. It is the 'I' that creates separation and superiority – even when it proclaims, 'I am in love!' It is the 'I' that contaminates every breath, demands our attention, and distracts us from the purity of the moment. It is the 'I' that rushes like a landslide over our Original Self, distorting the circle of our existence, preventing us from experiencing our essential nature: a human, being in love.

KM: Why do you call it the circle of our existence?

EK: Because the circle teaches that there is neither beginning nor end, there are no opposites, and there is only the thinnest dividing line between the so-called inside and the so-called outside.
I grew up in a round city. It was a city that valued its wisdom and protected its authority with seemingly impenetrable walls. As a boy, I saw the destruction of those walls. The shape of the city changed. Man-made cannot last. Man-made is invariably linear. The eternal circle is entirely different.

KM: In the June 1912 issue of our magazine we wrote 'Art...is the essential movement of Life.' What are your thoughts?

EK: Breath is the essential movement of life. How we use that breath might well be the highest art.

The Sayings of Epiah Khan

'Treat your name as a verb
rather than a noun;
whenever you say or hear it
remember you are a work in progress.'

* * *

'Watch every thought as if from a distance;
ask yourself,
"Shall I attach other thoughts to this?"'

* * *

'Train your imagination as you would a dog;
let it run free only when you know
it will return at your first command.'

* * *

'Knowledge is a prison,
subtle as a summer breeze that burns unnoticed;
wisdom is the freedom to travel beyond the furthest horizon.'

* * *

'Words travel on the breath;
so Nature teaches us
how to breathe well
before
we learn how to speak.'

'Friends give without expecting anything in return.
Friends know without being told.
Friendship is a language beyond words.'

* * *

'Time spent alone is a luxury
to those who share their lives with loved ones
and a prison sentence
to those who do not know they are loved.'

* * *

'If you find yourself in a hole of someone else's making,
you are either careless or dead.
If you are in a hole of your own making,
you are heading in the wrong direction.
Measure people not by how confidently they walk the streets,
but how well they climb out of a hole.'

* * *

'In a field that lacks commitment, excuses grow.'

* * *

'Too often Man decorates the world
through the strength of his will
and the flatulence of his Ego.'

'A spider's power lies in its web.
Be like a spider, develop your own web.'

* * *

'Attention is a gift to be given freely and without reservation.
When we fail to give attention,
the chains in our life fit, like belts,
around our spiritual waste.'

* * *

'Seek to overcome the perception that is
wrapped in assumption
veiled in intellect
viewed as truth.'

* * *

'Choose wisely
- you find what you search for.'

* * *

'The human intellect cannot be used to fathom God
anymore than a banana can be used to peel an orange;
choose the right tool for each task.'

'The man who fails to develop his intellect is stupid;
the man who fails to develop his heart is blind.'

* * *

'You gain experience through action.
You gain insight through contemplation.'

* * *

'If you are doing everything right
because you think that guarantees the right result,
you are doing everything right for the wrong reason.'

* * *

'Whenever the sun appears to shine over a new day,
there is no such thing as a conclusion.'

* * *

'Just as a book is far more than the number of pages the
writer fills
so the world is far more than the categories we create.
Learn to dissolve the categories
just as you learned to move seamlessly from one page to
another.'

'Things lost recently
are always close;
resist the temptation to search other rooms.'

* * *

'Thoughts pass through your mind
as clouds drift through the sky.
The sky is not the clouds.
You are not your thoughts.'

* * *

'The Almighty sees behind closed doors.'

* * *

'The Second Self acts as a veil between the soul and the
Almighty.
Two cannot become one whilst a veil exists between them.'

* * *

'Make your senses bright
then teach them to surrender.'

* * *

'Only that which is truly great can become truly small.'

'Silence is the mother of all communication.'

* * *

'If you journey to the place where your thoughts begin,
who do you find there?'

* * *

'Learn how to live through every part of your body;
know when to disregard each completely.'

* * *

'The source of a river is easier to find than the intention of
man.'

* * *

'When you truly feel the Earth beneath your feet
and the Heavens above you,
you have closed an important gap.'

* * *

'Words cannot exist on a page without space around them.
What is the page on which your thoughts exist?
What is the space around them?'

'A mirror, no matter how bright,
reflects only what stands before it.
The human heart, polished in silence,
reflects the unseen.'

* * *

'When you choose to attach meaning to a thought or action,
recognise the well from which the meaning springs.'

* * *

'How many times when you offer an opinion
rather than ask a question,
is it a sign of your uncertainty or Ego?'

* * *

'Contemplate in stillness;
act in silence;
be thankful always.'

* * *

'If you want to share your beliefs, speak;
when you want to test your faith, act.'

'When you celebrate your strengths,
they become your weaknesses.'

* * *

'Only when you truly accept that you can
fall, fail, cry, lose and hurt
as easily as anyone else
are you ready to submit to Greatness.'

* * *

'With whose eyes do you see?
With whose ears do you hear?
With whose hands do you feel?
Where is your heart?'

* * *

'Only the Second Self can be taken by surprise.'

* * *

'Winning is not a divine concept.'

'Celebrate everything you have;
understand you own nothing.
Only a person with nothing to lose can recognise a divine
message.'

* * *

'A strong man feels himself invincible.
The wise man makes himself invisible.'

* * *

'Every word you speak ripples throughout the world
moving it.'

* * *

'When I say "I love you"
and
You say "I know"
we are so far apart.'

* * *

'It is impossible to care truly for others if you need them to
like you.'

'Everyone can tell others what they know.
Few question
and learn
with eloquence and precision.
There are few true leaders.'

* * *

'Words can kill. How often do you forget that?
Words can heal. How often do you remember that?
Words are best formed in silence. How often do you do that?'

* * *

'The world is filled with distractions
– all man-made.'

* * *

'In the midst of the forest the oldest, strongest tree does
nothing to declare its presence;
it simply grows imperceptibly in silence.'

* * *

"There is hidden treasure
within you
around you
- look below the surface!'

'A man's fear shrinks the Universe
to the size of his own imagination.'

* * *

'Love is the spark that lights
the fire of courage.'

* * *

'Seek to achieve the irresistible power that comes only from
weakness.'

* * *

'Power comes from weakness
when you close the gap
between two hands.'

* * *

'We cannot be truly gracious
or offer genuine gratitude
until we are grace-full.'

'Between the certainty of "Yes" and the certainty of "No"
lies the invitation to Learn.'

* * *

'Whenever you have to make a decision,
determine accurately both the time you have in which to
analyse
and the time you have in which to act;
use both precisely.'

* * *

'To give and expect nothing in return
is true generosity.
To give in any other way is to secretly seek reward.'

* * *

'What defines you?
Is it what you choose to do
or what you choose *not* to do?'

* * *

'Reality exists in the space between two people.'

'The discovery the Scientist has not yet made we call Magic!
Magic is all around us…'

* * *

'The smallest thing can contain all,
just as the heart of a circle
is disguised as the very tip of a triangle.'

* * *

'Only by sharing your harvest
do you create space for a new crop to grow.'

* * *

'Opposites are never poles apart;
rather they exist nestled next to each other
on the circumference of a circle.'

* * *

'Every breath is a communication.'

'The level of peace in a person's life
is determined by the quality
of their most secret communication.'

* * *

'When you see a person fall
catch them in the first instance;
the longer you wait,
the more momentum they gain,
the more difficult it is to stop them from collapsing totally.'

* * *

'You must study with ferocity if you are to be worthy of your
suffering.'

* * *

'The most powerful sense
is non-sense.'

* * *

'Choose destruction over creativity at every opportunity;
destroy the Second Self!'

'Just as expansion cannot exist without contraction,
so it is only possible to grow by becoming small.'

* * *

'Whenever you have the opportunity to offer an opinion,
consider first
whether you should ask a question instead.'

* * *

'The heart longs to be shared.
Listen to it. Trust it.
Give it away and it will shine.
The heart's song is stronger than any pain.'

* * *

'Sometimes we feel a pain and give it life
because we think of a consequence we fear.'

* * *

'You can only make a true commitment
when you have nothing in your grasp.'

'You see a crescent moon in the night sky and know
it is only a matter of time before it reveals itself completely.
In the same way know that your heart is full,
even if you cannot yet feel it.'

* * *

'The empty cup does not know what will be placed within it,
nor can it influence that.
To be prepared
and true to one's nature
we must be empty of the non-essential.'

* * *

'We cannot give love if we are too close.'

* * *

'We have more space in which to grow
than we can possibly imagine.'

* * *

'If you are searching for the Divine
search now!
Here!
Search in the instant!'

'The future cannot be known
any more than it can be controlled.
Peace exists only in the moment.'

* * *

'We can only breathe one breath at a time.
Understand the lesson in this.'

* * *

'Seek unknowing rather than knowing.
Find joy in ignorance!'

* * *

'The Devil hides
within
the complexity of expertise,
the warm cloak of power,
the attraction of others,
the false promises of tomorrow.'

* * *

'To sacrifice oneself for a person we love
is a selfish act;
To sacrifice oneself for a person we will never know
is a selfless act.'

'Go ever into the Darkness,
silently, empty, searching.
Yearning!'

* * *

'The flower grows silently,
reaching for the Heavens
it's roots deep in Mother Earth;
be like the flower!'

* * *

'There is only one thing of value a teacher can teach
and a student can learn:
how to let go of the Second Self.'

* * *

'The most powerful force
is not a bayonet,
nor a bullet nor a bomb.
The most powerful force is Love.
Only Love destroys completely.'

* * *

'Silence accepts, allows, absorbs;
silence is the transforming home of opposites.'

'Distil everything down into the smallest word.
A single syllable is at the heart of all language,
in the beat of every heart.'

* * *

'To be truly rich one must learn how to travel well,
how to close the gap between one's self and others.'

* * *

'Balance is only truly understood by those used to travelling
on the edge.'

* * *

'Are you being uniquely yourself?
If not, who are you being?'

* * *

'Success and failure are attitudes,
not outcomes.'

'Stillness is not stagnation,
movement is not growth,
experience is not learning;
purpose, passion and sacrifice are essential if value is to be
created.'

* * *

'When you grow yourself and then reach out to others
you provide nourishment and support.
Be hungry for growth,
be strong enough to reach out.'

* * *

'When you say a person is wearing blinkers,
you are acknowledging only that they are wearing
different blinkers to your own.'

* * *

'Learn how to listen,
learn how to look,
only then are you ready to learn how to speak.'

* * *

'Great teachers help others discover
what they are ready to learn.'

'Engineers shape our world;
teachers fill in all the spaces.'

* * *

'Words are as sharp as swords,
as explosive as bombs;
release with care.'

* * *

'Only challenge the beliefs and ideas of others
if you are continually challenging your own.'

* * *

'Long to be
in the instant
without separation;
long to *be*
and perhaps
- perhaps -
if only for for a heartbeat
you will belong
completely.'

* * *

'Understanding is the best of all reasons
to say
"No".'

'Teachers teach by their example:
sharing their weaknesses as well as their strengths.'

* * *

'You can always choose where to look;
you can always choose what to remember.'

* * *

'Silence is the space in which awareness and connectivity
grow.'

* * *

'The body reveals the mind.'

* * *

'You can measure the quality of a Society
by the quality of the Service its people provide.'

* * *

'Everything created deliberately begins with belief.'

'Power is a burden not a gift.
It can only be carried well by those
strong enough to subdue the Second Self.'

* * *

'Love is neither a gift nor a reward.
Love is supreme forgetfulness.
Love is selfless surrender.'

* * *

'Our capacity for insight and connection
is matched only by our capacity
for self-deception.'

* * *

'In your thoughts
and your spoken words
seek to avoid
the "I" of Isolation.'

* * *

'When you spread ashes
always be clear which way the wind is blowing.'

'All thought,
if developed to its absolute conclusion,
leads back
to the nakedness of the beginning.'

* * *

'The things we leave behind
are the things those who follow us
begin with.'

* * *

'The act itself
is as nothing compared to the Source.'

* * *

'Never answer the question until it is asked;
realise there are many ways it can be asked.'

* * *

'Treated well, beliefs dissolve
into
Mystery.'

'It isn't the word that matters;
it's what the word does that matters.'

* * *

'The Mystery is ever-present,
calling, deepening into the instant;
too often our ears are deaf.'

* * *

'We can draw only from the depths we have been to.'

* * *

'Breath connects the outside and the inside,
breaking down barriers and boundaries,
daring us to let go.'

* * *

'Words are sounds reverberating in silence
- listen to the silence, not the words.'

'Whatever we do
wherever we go
we leave things behind
always.'

* * *

'Tread carefully,
the solidity of the edge
is always next to the emptiness of the fall.'

* * *

'The patterns we return to
weave the picture of our life.'

* * *

'Sometimes when the teacher shines
light into the darkness,
the light blinds.'

* * *

'It is best to treat yourself as you treat others:
sometimes you don't listen to what others are saying
or realise what they are thinking,
sometimes you don't notice them,
sometimes you forget them completely.'

'Everything has to be somewhere.'

* * *

'Will is desire
manifested and directed continually
until the objective is achieved.'

* * *

'The horizon exists
to remind our eyes to see the heavens
and our feet to feel the Earth.'

* * *

'The silence whispers,
"Every word paints a thousand pictures." ' [3]

---

[3] The phrase, 'Use a picture. It's worth a thousand words.' was first used by Tess Flanders, editor of the Syracuse Post-Standard in the March 28th 1911 edition of the newspaper. It is unclear whether Epiah Khan was aware of it.

'Every belief that supports or grows the Ego
is the worst of man-made.'

* * *

'The word "No"
is best reached through
the gateway of "Yes".'

* * *

'Suffering and Love
survive only within the shadow of the other
- an invisible bond.'

* * *

'Silence and Stillness
are methods, not goals;
misunderstood
they become as seductive as the warmest blankets.'

* * *

'Human culture is
the consequence and creation
of
the Collective Ego.'

'Memories are walls,
some beautiful to behold,
others serving as prisons;
ignore the walls
- find the door!'

* * *

'To be truly Present
is to experience the Presence.'

* * *

'Before it is ever a solution
war
is always a sign of failure.'

* * *

'You have to earn the right
to gain insight and understanding,
best to earn the right joyously!'

'There are no miracles,
only unexpected experiences
offering deeper insights,
greater challenges to beliefs,
opportunities for the heart to be heard.'

* * *

'Words
like bones
are left behind;
easy to forget
in the swill of sound.'

* * *

'Storage alone is never proof of care or need.'

* * *

'I have to get past me to get to you;
Love lights the way.'

* * *

'The power of an army
is measured
by the strength of its warriors' tears.'

'I think
therefore
I am not in the Present.'[4]

* * *

'There is something hidden in the wind
something transformed and transforming
a part of it is you,
a part of it is me.'

* * *

'Knowing + not knowing = love and faith.
The perfect equation.'

* * *

'We learn through community
- even when alone.'

---

[4] René Descartes' well-known phrase, 'I think therefore I am', written in
Latin as 'Cogito ergo sum' and in French as 'je pense, donc je suis'
appeared in his work *Discourse on the Method* in 1637.

'Nature has no plan.
She leaves that to us.'

* * *

'Give yourself up to the inevitability of success,
everyone becomes great at something.'

* * *

'Care enough to be curious.
Love enough to risk.'

* * *

'There are always teachers in your life;
if you can't see them,
take out your eyes
and begin again.'

* * *

'Avoid separation
between what you do
and
who you are.'

'The darkness is an invitation,
accept it and engage.'

* * *

'Walk when others rest,
be silent when others speak,
be awake when others sleep,
pray always.'

* * *

'Repetition
is a falsehood
wrapped in the falsehood of time
mapped in the falsehood of memory
used as the building block of unhelpful stories.'

* * *

'The prison of *I*
with its soot-black walls
and constant chatter
deafens inmates.'

* * *

'Habits long to be fed;
fasting is the cure.'

'Forget whoever you think you are;
meet with joy whoever remains.'

* * *

'Without surrender
it will be a long time
before we are children again.'

* * *

'The family that keeps its net
cast firmly around its members
kills the heart.'

* * *

'Where should you look in order to see the intention of
others?
Look over their shoulders,
into the Universe.'

* * *

'The most peaceful resting place
is
Mystery.'

'Whenever you cry, study your tears;
they always contain both sorrow and joy.'

* * *

'As your commitment grows
so does your love
and your vulnerability
- such joyous weakness!'
'The word "Yes"
has more depths
than the deepest ocean.'

* * *

'Thoughts are thunder in the storm of the mind,
they drown all other sounds;
impossible, then, to think and listen at the same time.'

* * *

'Study secretly,
lose yourself in your learning,
a student's silence defeats the Second Self.'

* * *

'Avoid clinging;
learn how to process.'

'To escape the body,
to live – even for one second –
on the other side of our skin.
What freedom!'

* * *

'Communities fracture
whenever culture tightens,
just as relationships break
whenever trust disappears.'

* * *

'The ocean does not own the fish or the waves.
The earth does not own the mountains or wind.
The night sky does not own the moon or the stars.
What do *you* own?'

* * *

'When boundaries become blockages
inflammation builds
until poison bursts.'

* * *

'Treat your body as clothing
- a changeable covering
that isn't you.'

'Thoughts are the tools that shape our world;
make them bright and sharp,
use with precision,
disregard with ease.'

* * *

'Every time you take a breath
you are reaching into the Universe,
just as a child dips her toes into a fast-flowing stream.'

* * *

'There are four pillars to learning and living well.
They are Faith, Dedication, Sincerity and Willpower.'

* * *

'Avoid communities that suggest superiority
avoid brotherhood that builds borders
- belonging mismanaged makes ever-tightening walls
inevitable.'

* * *

'When you learn to be comfortable with Mystery
you learn to be comfortable with yourself,
the home of the greatest Mystery.'

'What is the difference between Time and Space?
One depends upon language for its existence.'

* * *

'Words are guides
pointing to something beyond their simple sound;
too often we treat them as cages
containing a specific reality.'

* * *

'The sheath is more important than the blade,
the frame more important than the painting,
silence more important than sound.'

* * *

'Love is a Mystery.
Follow your heart!
Run towards the Mystery!
Run! Now!'

* * *

'Look at every person you meet
as if you are looking into a mirror;
only speak when you see at least a part of yourself
reflected there.'

'Imagine if all your thoughts were reduced to one,
if you could think only one thought for the rest of your life,
what would it be?'

* * *

'Intention is formed on the in-breath,
revealed on the out-breath;
in the space between
the Universe waits,
open,
judgement-free.'

* * *

'Life is an empty house;
yours to fill as you choose.'

* * *

'The palette of your mind
colours your senses;
paint a new picture every day!'

* * *

'Avoid going for a walk through the forest;
rather spend time *being* in the forest.'

'The best reason for climbing a mountain
is to learn how to fall from a greater height.'

* * *

'Avoid the teacher who emphasises
solutions rather than movement
reasons rather then metaphor
information rather than myth,
they cannot prepare you for the inevitable fall.'

* * *

'Learn how to recognise the difference between
the container
and
the contents.'

* * *

'Wisdom straddles borders,
it is never found on one side alone.'

* * *

'Surrender precedes awareness;
the more joyful the surrender,
the more insightful the moment.'

'Whenever we fall
Mother Earth catches us,
offering the roots of rebirth.'

* * *

'Eyes cannot see
and ears cannot hear
when the heart is blocked.'

* * *

'Signposts point the way
without hesitation,
without asking for permission,
without debate.
We are all signposts.
In which direction are you pointing?'

* * *

'The first response when you meet a teacher
is to lower yourself,
the second response is to lower yourself,
the third response is to lower yourself;
the more completely the seed is buried,
the more chance it has to grow.'

'The logical argument, easy to accept,
is as real and true as the soil on the surface of the planet;
far beneath it, the core burns
- the searing truth of the heart!'

* * *

'Everything man-made is the result of personal desire
and negotiation,
everything else is the result of a silent, eternal process;
only silence lasts.'

* * *

'Distance is an illusion
explored best through stillness.'

* * *

'In order to go beyond,
one must first go inward.'

* * *

'People living on the other side of our planet
are less than half a step away
in the grand space of the Universe.'

'You cannot create the connection
- only uncover it.'

* * *

'The best of leaders
are servants first
fighters last
egotists never.'

* * *

'It is easier to fear, hate and fight
than to see the humanity we share with others;
avoid those so-called leaders
who
despise difference
develop distrust
delight in division.'

* * *

'The Wisdom of the Village
is the eternal knowledge
shared by elders lost in learning
with nothing to prove;
without them Society crumbles.'

'Ensure every challenge you face,
everything you do,
peels away the Second Self.'

* * *

'The greatest freedom
begins
with
freedom from beliefs.'

* * *

'Massage Mother Earth with your footsteps
wrap her in your breath
feed her with your smile.'

* * *

'The wrapping around the present,
no matter how appealing,
always has to be removed.'

* * *

'Whenever a beginning and an ending touch
a new circle is formed.'

'The lesson is simple:
Hear and Now.'

* * *

'The beginning is always much closer to the end than we
think;
too soon we realise how little time and space separate them.'

* * *

'Learn what is good from your education then leave;
learn what is good from your family then leave;
learn what is good from your Society then leave;
learn what is good from the world
return home and share it all.
Then leave.'

* * *

'Even when there are no thoughts
the residue of
experience, interpretation and imagination
remain
layered
in the silence.'

'When the hearts beats
the body vibrates,
the universe expands;
Life's opportunities more numerous than the stars.'

* * *

'If you let go of the stories you carry
all that is left
filling the Space
is
the first Truth.'

* * *

''Thoughts nestle next to Silence on the
circumference of communication;
only when you have experienced fully
the long journey between them
can you appreciate their intimate connection.'

* * *

'The Second Self feeds on transaction
whilst the Original Self fasts.'

'Mystery is both joyous and challenging.
The joy is that Mystery is layered endlessly,
the challenge is that the next layer is always available.'

* * *

'You are like the river.
Born pure, moved inside and out,
filling over time with both new life and debris.
The Almighty is the current,
sometime obvious,
often not,
ensuring timeless flow always.'

* * *

'When you wake in the night
with your thoughts tumbling
let them go
like raindrops from a cloud;
when you wake in the night
and the Darkness calls
answer
swift as lightening!'

* * *

'When Death approaches
look over its shoulders.'

'Faith is not a well-fitting suit;
there are times it is uncomfortable to wear.'

* * *

'The determined, consistent, ever-curious student
forces the teacher to appear.'

* * *

'The neutral point, free from expectation,
is the birthplace of curiosity and insight.'

* * *

'Comparison is the recognition of difference;
unhealthy comparison is when that recognition is used to
diminish oneself or others.'

* * *

'When you ask a question, you reveal yourself;
have the courage to be naked in pursuit of your learning.'

'When you hear the sound of the Universe,
when you feel its rhythm,
everything becomes a dance.'

* * *

'Only those things that are man-made can be changed;
Nature simply flows.'

* * *

'Boundaries mark difference,
make entry and exit difficult,
represent established power and rules;
most of all, they limit learning.
It is impossible to grow
- and impossible to love -
unless you are open.'

* * *

'The lioness hunts without fear;
consequence cannot limit her;
no sound or movement can distract her.
When you decide to learn,
hunt with the single-minded ferocity of the lioness.'

'When a valued guest knocks on your door,
you welcome them in.
Your Heart is the door to your Original Self,
seek entry,
empty the rooms,
find Peace.'

* * *

'Learn how to breathe well in the darkness;
walk bravely, blind, with a caring disregard for the Second
Self.'

* * *

'Love without thought!
Love without reason!
Love without knowing!
Love!'

* * *

'Nothing is hidden from those who know how to see.'

* * *

'Temptation draws us to look out of the window
judging what we see
without a thought for our own rooms.'

'Better to find the light within,
to feel its heat,
to know its challenge,
than to fuel the Second Self
by only shining light for others.'

* * *

'In the darkness of the Village
Wisdom waits.'

* * *

'The Answer is never hidden.
Rather, like the mountain top
and the ocean bed,
it waits for those who seek out pressure.'

* * *

'Look at the Space
rather than the objects within it,
then – perhaps – you will begin to see
the Universe
flowing endlessly.'

'Listen to Silence
rather than the sounds it carries,
then – perhaps – you will begin to hear
the Universe
calling you home.'

* * *

'Mystery is not a puzzle to be solved,
or an answer to be found;
Mystery is Life, Union, Loss.'

* * *

'If you truly want to learn,
study until there are no words left,
then surrender to your heart.'

* * *

'The rope, laid lengthways, has both beginning and end.
Once knotted, the same rope reveals itself as a circle.
There can be no revelation until the knot is tied.'

'There is only One Breath;
give yourself to it,
draw deeply,
let it take you,
transport you,
Home.'

* * *

'Silence carries sound
just as the ocean carries waves.
Seek the silent current,
not the crash and thunder.'

* * *

'Beware the thieves,
disguised as thoughts,
that come to steal your treasure.
Dispel them with your breath.'

* * *

'Never look directly when giving attention.
Instead let your eyes find their own place,
silence the rooms within,
and wait for words
that are not of your creation
to move your mouth.'

'Comparison is man-made
and always filled with risk.
Nature never compares.
She does not know how.'

* * *

'Listen to your own words
more than you do the words of others.
Review your own words
more than you do those of others.
Your words reveal where you are.
They signal where you must go next.'

* * *

'When you are at peace,
when you are truly peaceful,
every room is emptied of the man-made.
The peaceful home has no boundaries.'

* * *

'Ignore the deceit of distance.
It exists only when you look outward.'

* * *

'In the silence of the home,
the heart shares its message,
names its desire.'

'Breath reaches further than the hands,
touches more than skin,
shares more than sound.
Love creates the breath.
Love travels on the breath.
Breathe from your heart.'

* * *

'You cannot make a connection with others,
you can only recognise that it already exists.'

* * *

'The Second Self can never win the race;
sometimes that is only realised in the final steps.'

* * *

'Seek out and rejoice in the little deaths;
they are our footprints in the sands of time.'

* * *

'Those who deny, degrade, or despise us
offer profound lessons.
Be grateful to them.'

'Remember this:
there is no such thing as a
passive movement;
inside or out.'

* * *

'Nature never creates prisons
- they are always man-made.'

* * *

'The sharper the blade,
the less the edge exists;
the closer we come to perfection,
the more we disappear.'

* * *

'One does not demonstrate knowledge
by the answers they give,
but by the questions they ask.'

* * *

'Avoid the teacher who talks more loudly
and more frequently
than all the rest.
Rather,
seek the teacher who knows how to breathe knowledge
into your heart.'

'The circumference marks the circle;
it does not reveal the pen.
And the pen cannot reveal
the dot at the centre of the circle.'

* * *

The Circles in your Life
'Ensure that:

Caution isn't cowardice
Humility isn't fear
Knowledge isn't the purpose
Mistakes are not failures
Success is not resolution
Perception is not mistaken for reality
Love is not explained
Causes are not isolated
Words are not answers.

And then make:

Space the medium you manage
Time the wave you ride
Your gaze far-reaching
Your vision bright
Your purpose irresistible.

Make:

Learning fun
Uncertainty exciting
Happiness infectious

Gratitude instinctive
and
Peace your gift.

As the knots loosen, travel, and celebrate the circles in your
life.'

* * *

I once knew a man
'I once knew a man who only remembered the sun when it
burnt his skin.
He only gave to charity when a hand reached out.
He only laughed when someone told him a funny story.
When his physician said he was seriously ill, he collapsed and
died.'

* * *

'I once knew a man who said he practiced medicine to make
people better.
He never did.
At best, he simply took their illness away.
He never made anyone *better*.'

'I once knew a teacher who taught everyone he met.
He spent so much time teaching he forgot how to learn.
Eventually the gap between himself and his students became
so great
it could not be crossed
even by a leap of faith.'

* * *

'I once knew a writer who argued that words defined reality.
When he finished talking I kicked him silently in the groin.'

* * *

'I once knew a man who suffered many tragedies.
The greatest of all was
that he managed his pain and loss successfully
only
to be drowned in the sympathy of others.'

* * *

'I once knew a man who said he was a selfless teacher,
yet he was desperate to help others change.'

* * *

'I once knew a man who never thought of himself;
I asked him why he laughed so much.
He told me why he cried.'

Influence

'When you need to engage the intellect of another
Apply your intellect;
When you need to engage the body of another
Move your body;
When you need to touch the heart of another
breathe words from your heart.'

* * *

Suspense

'The space between the question and the answer,
the touch and the response,
the intention and the outcome,
the space between the beginning and the end of everything,
is filled with suspense.
More than anything else, life is Suspense-full;
learn to love it.'

* * *

Opposites (i)

'We live in a world of apparent Opposites
Men and women
Night and day
Land and sea
Right and wrong
Action and inaction.
The challenge is how to recognise and respond to these
without being pulled apart.
Unity exists only when there is no separation.'

Opposites (ii)
'Even opposites come from a single, most natural point.
There – before they separate – they are one.
At birth and at death these opposites reunite.
Our challenge, during the fullness of life, is to close the gap,
to uncover that most natural place,
to experience the world from that perspective.'

* * *

The Unknown
'More than anything else, we must reveal the unknown.
When people say they are afraid of the unknown they mean
those things they cannot imagine
or do not understand.
That is why some are afraid of the dark,
some are afraid to travel,
some are afraid of strangers.
I wonder, Do they know *who* is afraid?'

* * *

Experience
'Escape the mind – experience the body.
Escape the body – experience the horizon.
Escape the horizon – experience space.
Enter into space – experience love.
Experience love – experience everything.'

Enemies

'When your enemy is powerful and approaches forcefully,
celebrate your own weakness and move to one side – you will
gain a new perspective.
When your enemy appears weak and unprepared, ensure you
can see both his hands clearly - then defeat him from a
distance.
When your enemy insists he is your friend, connect the past
to the future – you will find your answer there.
When you are sure you have no enemies to face, look inside –
there you will find the home of them all.'

* * *

The Teacher

'Sometimes I teach by saying or doing less than expected.
Sometimes I teach by saying or doing more than expected.
Sometimes I teach by saying or doing the unexpected.
Only rarely do I teach by saying or doing what is expected.'

* * *

Not enough

'It is not enough to ask a question,
you have to seek the answer.
It is not enough to hold a belief,
you must challenge it constantly.
It is not enough to lay claim to a faith,
you need to exercise it openly in the face of adversity.'

A Casual Glance
'So many people offer the world nothing more than a casual
glance,
they see only a glimmer of all that is around and within them.
Based on that
they create their beliefs,
make their decisions
shape their lives;
with only a glimmer to inform them
they convince the next generation of the truths
that must be upheld
in order to justify their own behaviour.'

* * *

The Essence
'There is a point at the centre of a circle,
that contains all that is around it.
It is the Essence.
When you look at another, look to their Essence.
When you speak, speak to their Essence.
When you listen, listen to what their Essence is telling you.
Everything else is just clutter inside their circumference.'

Opening and Closing

'When you wake in the morning:
breathe in the air of the new day,
feel the heavens above you,
feel the earth beneath your feet,
then share your love.
Begin each day well.

Before you sleep at night:
share your love;
feel the earth beneath your feet;
then feel the heavens above you.
Sleep well.'

* * *

Pain

'There are three types of pain:
pain of the Body
pain of the Ego
pain of the Secret Heart.
Pain of the Body can be acted upon or ignored according to
circumstance.
Pain of the Ego should be encouraged and developed until it
is unbearable.
The pain of the Secret Heart is beyond words.'

The River

'The water in the river does not stay near the source from
which it springs;
it is moved by the current
transforming and changing
across lands
into seas and oceans.
We are that water
born
pure
close to the source.
And then we are taken
spinning and rushing
ever further away.
To return,
to be at one with the source,
we have to let go of everything that was not there in that first
instant.'

Senses
'Brighten your eyes so they see every colour.
Train your ears so they hear the quietest of sounds.
Soften your feet so they feel Mother Earth.
Enliven your mouth so all flavours are clear.
Breathe so you can recognise the most delicate of perfumes.
And then know,
that no matter how bright your vision,
how acute your hearing,
how soft your feet,
how lively your mouth,
how sensitive your nose,
they will never experience the Almighty.
That is the domain of the Secret Heart.'

* * *

The Library
'We carry stories deep within ourselves;
they are the stories
through which we carry our past,
experience the present and imagine the future.
Some of these stories are our own creation,
some are the work of others.
Write and accept the stories in your life with care,
the library inside you determines the Universe you inhabit.'

Challenges
'Some challenges are the result of our weakness,
take ownership and use them to grow.
Some challenges are life's gift
created beyond our control,
welcome them as unasked for lessons.
Some challenges are hard-earned,
the result of our endeavour,
celebrate them.'

* * *

First
'What precedes Action?
Intention.
What precedes Intention?
Awareness.
What precedes Awareness?
Breath.
What precedes Breath?
The First Intention.'

* * *

Silence
'The cure for all addiction is love.
The source of all love is willing surrender.
The reason for surrender is joyous weakness.
The lesson hidden in joyous weakness is peace.
The value of peace is unity.
When unity is felt comparisons end.
When comparisons end there is greater silence.
In greater silence there only *Is*.'

Living in the Moment

'If you believe you are living in the moment
you are not;
if you feel you are living in the moment
you are not;
if you say you are living in the moment
you are not;
when the moment takes you
you are not.'

The Rubaiyat of Epiah Khan

This collection ends with Epiah Khan's only known poem. Essentially it follows the structure and rhythms of a rubaiyat. However, Epiah plays with the structure, adding his own unique style to create a sense of flow and points of emphasis.

The poem is an allegory, describing one man's search to uncover his Original Self.

The Rubaiyat of Epiah Khan

1.
He woke after a dream-filled sleep
the memories he tried to keep;
they teased and slipped back to the night.
He wondered if perhaps they'd seep

2.
into the morning Winter light
where Nature shed and dared delight,
where life withdrew or burrowed down
and rainbow colours disappeared from sight.

3.
He felt the snow, crisp on the ground;
he walked and heard its unique sound.
The sky was clear with hidden threat;
he thought he smiled – in truth, he frowned.

4.
The day had come his mind was set,
there was no turning back – and yet
his imagination sought to make him stall
spurred by the feeling he could not forget:

5.
the pressure of the shadow-wall;
how it absorbed his every call
and, like a mask, it turned him blind
and, like a wire, it made him fall

6.
into the darkness of his mind
where hope and faith were left behind,
where monsters roamed the wilderness
- such wild things not of his kind.

7.
They filled his heart with great distress;
they scored it with each sharp caress,
reminding him he was their home;
their strength increased as his grew less.

8.
And shackled there he heard them roam.
He was their prisoner, trapped alone,
without belief or sense of grace;
inside himself, the great unknown.

9.
So, in the present, he kept his pace
and forced his thoughts from out that place,
as Winter's chill bit at his skin
and flakes of snow fell on his face.

10.
Time for the journey to begin
to leave behind his charred chagrin,
to fasten dogs to empty sled
to go without and not within.

11.
Hórama was the one who led.
The keenest eyes to look ahead,
with vision searching bright and clear
to find the route with nothing said.

12.
Akoúō next, who knew no fear.
No matter what, would always hear
the sounds Nature sought to conceal;
she heard them all, the sharpest ear.

13.
Háptó came third, at his sister's heel,
strong of touch, able to feel
the changing ground or the devil's spell,
he shared them both with equal zeal.

14.
And then ran *Osmé*, whose nose so well
sought every scent and every smell,
close to the ground where'er they raced
each subtle perfume she could tell.

15.
Geûma last, in perfect place,
an open mouth, ready to taste
every flavour he could find.
The man knew he was truly graced.

16.
Five dogs whose qualities combined,
his sense of Self was thus defined.
He gave them power to lead the way
whilst some part else was lost behind.

17.
They raced ahead without delay.
The sled – named *Phren* – forced to obey
every command the dogs did send;
the man's face fixed firm into Winter's grey.

18.
This journey toward an unknown end
the place, he prayed, he could transcend
the monsters roaming wild and free,
those forces he could not contend.

19.
He had been warned, 'No guarantee -
Nature might force you to your knee.
'Tis human folly to be sure
when journey's end you cannot foresee.'

20.
'I will,' he said, 'accept, endure
all trials that might help secure
the freedom I so truly seek
I will avoid the lie and lure.'

21.
He wondered if he would ever speak
again to those he'd kissed upon the cheek
his fond farewell, his last goodbye,
as the clouds came low, the weather bleak.

22.
And so they ran beneath a weighted sky,
on the dogs and sled he could rely
to carry him to the wilderness,
where no nearby Saviour would hear his cry.

23.
Alone to face such dark distress,
his burning heart in the great furnace
- the fire and flames of the deep Not-Knowing,
his one defence, his wilfulness.

24.
Hórama strong, with bright eyes glowing,
the other four, no sign of slowing,
away from everything man-made,
into the perfect storm, the overflowing.

25.
Then darkness crushed - he was dismayed
to feel its presence, how it weighed
so dense upon his soul's desire,
the light now gone from his crusade.

26.
At once, he felt his life force tire,
Phren held him now as if a pyre.
He wondered if he might have died.
He listened for an angel choir.

27.
He heard no sounds; he saw no guide.
He called for help; no voice replied.
The dark squeezed tight; he fought for air.
He could not move; he could not hide.

28.
The dogs had gone; he knew not where.
Not wilful now – filled with despair;
the promise lost of victory.
His heart released a silent prayer.

29.
He had no name, no history,
no memories, no-thing that he
could hold on fast and call his own.
The monsters hid the mystery:

30.
the dark the place to move the stone,
to free those monsters he had grown,
the place where senses cannot go
where man bows down and must atone.

31.
His knees on earth, his forehead low,
he surrendered to the wind and snow,
to the never-ending reach of Space
to all above and all below.

32.
He felt the tears run down his face,
of the man he was, no more a trace,
less, and beyond, the greatest word
before his eyes, all life embraced.

33.
The final blessing then transferred,
an awareness for the first time stirred,
of what his heart had always yearned.
The vision stopped; silence was heard.

34.
He felt as if he had been burned
and deep inside some part had turned,
the first of all, never once alone.
He knew, at last, he had returned

35.
Home.

Printed in Poland
by Amazon Fulfillment
Poland Sp. z o.o., Wrocław
28 March 2023

b2be27e1-f1fe-4ff0-b235-3ba7b29fbdadR01